Barbie™

First published in Great Britain 2023 by Expanse, a part of Farshore
An imprint of HarperCollins*Publishers*
1 London Bridge Street, London SE1 9GF
www.farshore.co.uk

HarperCollins*Publishers*
Macken House, 39/40 Mayor Street Upper,
Dublin 1 D01 C9W8, Ireland

Written by Malcolm Mackenzie

Images used under licence from Shutterstock.com.

ISBN 978 0 00 867171 6
Printed in Bosnia and Herzegovina
001

FSC™ C007454

This book is produced from independently certified FSC™ paper
to ensure responsible forest management.

For more information visit: www.harpercollins.co.uk/green

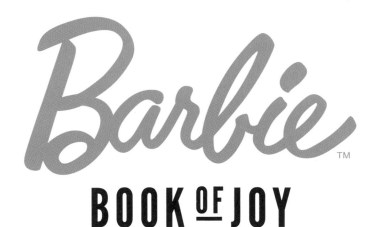

BOOK OF JOY

EXPANSE

INTRODUCTION

The first ever Barbie doll hit shelves in 1959 and she had impeccable style from the second her tiny toes touched the ground.

But Barbie is famously flexible and was never just about looking great. She was a go-getter from the get-go. In 1966 she launched herself into space and her career path has soared in all directions since then: from army sergeant to dentist, from pilot to the president.

She wants you to know that if you have a dream, pursue it, because if she can do it, so can you!

Barbie grows with her ever-changing audience, staying ahead of the latest trends, building new dreams and dream houses. The things that never change, no matter what, are Barbie doll's spirit of love and kindness, her openness to new experiences, curiosity and of course her desire to live outside the box.

This book guides you through today's world of Barbie, sharing her thoughts and philosophies, because Barbie is famous for her unshakeable optimism.

No matter what job she's doing that day, she is a ray of sunshine and an avatar of hope.

Everyone has their own Barbie era. The Barbie dolls that they saw in the toy shop. The ones they remember owning and loving. Today she returns our admiration with an infectious smile that says, "We can do anything. What's it going to be?"

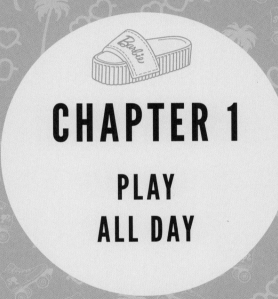

CHAPTER 1

PLAY
ALL DAY

" Sorry, can't make it.
I'm all booked up. "

" Making forever memories with my BFFs — **Best Festival Friends**. "

" Now this look
is a **slam dunk** —
sorry, wrong game,
I mean **total serve**. "

" I'm only stopping to **admire the view**. "

" Dreaming of being a DJ, then remembering the **2am start times**. Zzzzzzz. "

" **Sun, sand, sea** and holding onto your hat. "

" Take the picture,
this ice lolly hasn't
got **long to live**. "

" Squashing everyone on to my two-seater sofa for movie night? Challenge accepted. **Don't lose the remote!** "

"
Run as forest as you can. Hydrate. And **start all over again**.
"

" In order to **blossom**, you've got to **grow**. "

"The guidebook says that this is the best place to spot **mermaids**."

" **Sharing is caring,
unless ice cream
is involved.** "

CHAPTER 2

BE THE
BOSS

" Prioritising a comfy
workspace over a
**flattering camera
angle** for this
meeting. "

"

Every project starts with a vision and **a whole lot** of sticky tape. "

" Look, scrolling social media is **an essential part** of keeping up with the competition. "

" **Starting a new project when anything's possible** ... **and budgets have yet to be finalised.** "

" I was born to lead. "

" The **dream house** won't re-decorate itself. Swatch this space. "

"It's recommended that you **take a break** every 20 minutes."

" I'm not **not** an interior designer. "

" Finding the **best light**
for the video call. "

"**Bossing it in black,
just to keep people
on their toes**, y'know?"

CHAPTER 3

TOGETHER
WE SHINE

" Finally getting us out of the **group chat** and into the **group hang**. "

" Friends don't leave you **out in the cold.** "

" You can't make new old friends, **so treat them with extra special care.** "

" When you find the
perfect spot for subtle
people-watching. "

" The **golden hour** is every hour spent with you. "

" There's no mountain we can't **climb**. "

" Enjoy the journey,
share the ride,
but don't judge
my singing voice. "

"
Friendship is not fighting over the last piece of **red velvet cake**.
"

" The gang's keeping it cool in the **shade.** "

" Take the picture.
Nobody sneeze. "

" Friends are the family we **choose for ourselves.** "

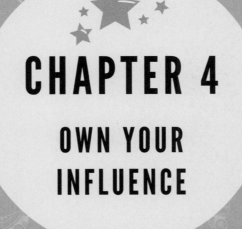

CHAPTER 4

OWN YOUR INFLUENCE

" **Good friends** go with everything. "

" Low-key
stopping traffic
since 1959. **"**

"It's not just a selfie, it's a **permanent record** of the perfect fringe."

" If you want **to be heard,** first you have **to be seen.** "

"Never tulle much,
never tulle much."

" Q: Dress or trousers?
A: Why not both?! "

" It's always **Fashion Week** somewhere. "

" Your friendly
reminder that
leopard print
is a neutral. "

" Look, if it rains, you can still see how **transparently fabulous** my outfit is. "

" Are you beginning **to see a pattern?** "

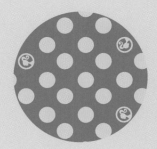

"
This old thing?
Oh, it's something I've had for aaaages.
"

"
Never dim
your sunshine.
"

CHAPTER 5

LOVE YOURSELF

"Sometimes **I keep it casual** and let my confidence do the styling."

" When **life gives you lemons**, squeeze them into your hair. "

" **Warrior one and two.**
That's all. "

" Self-care is letting **yourself** know how much you matter. "

" When a trip to the flower market calls for an **impromptu** photoshoot. "

"
Time to ride
your next wave.
"

" I thought you
said **dessert**,
not desert. "

" Turn your bathroom **into a spa-throom.** "

" When you want to put the phone down, **but need to see what the cat does next.** "

"
Buckets of charm,
with or without the hat.
"